C000088624

About the ITSM Library

The publications in the ITSM Library cover best practice in IT Management and are published on behalf of itSMF International (itSMF-I).

The IT Service Management Forum (itSMF) is the association for IT service organizations, and for customers of IT services. itSMF's goal is to promote innovation and support of IT management; suppliers and customers are equally represented within the itSMF. The Forum's main focus is exchange of peer knowledge and experience. Our authors are global experts.

The following publications are, or soon will be, available.

Introduction, Foundations and Practitioners books
- Foundations of IT Service Management based on ITIL® / IT Service Management – an introduction, based on ITIL® (Arabic, Chinese, Danish, German, English, French, Italian, Japanese, Korean, Dutch, Brazilian Portuguese, Russian, and Spanish)
- IT Services Procurement – an introduction based on ISPL (Dutch)
- Project Management based on PRINCE2 (Dutch, English, German)
- Practitioner Release & Control for IT Service Management, based on ITIL (English)

IT Service Management – best practices
- IT Service Management – best practices, part 1 (Dutch)
- IT Service Management – best practices, part 2 (Dutch)
- IT Service Management – best practices, part 3 (Dutch)
- IT Service Management – best practices, part 4 (Dutch)

Topics & Management instruments
- Metrics for IT Service Management (English)
- Six Sigma for IT Management (English)
- The RfP for IT Outsourcing (Dutch)
- Service Agreements – A Management Guide (English)
- Frameworks for IT Management (English, German, Japanese)

Pocket guides
- ISO/IEC 20000 – a pocket guide (English, German, Italian, Spanish, formerly BS 15000 – a pocket guide)
- IT Services Procurement based on ISPL – a pocket guide (English)
- IT Governance – a pocket guide based on CobiT (English, German)
- IT Governance based on CobiT4 - A Management Guide
- IT Service CMM – a pocket guide (English)
- IT Service Management – a summary based on ITIL® (Dutch)
- IT Service Management from hell! (English)

For any further enquiries about ITSM Library, please visit www.itsmfbooks.com, http://en.itsmportal.net/books.php?id=35 or www.vanharen.net.

ISO/IEC 20000

A POCKET GUIDE

Van Haren
PUBLISHING

Colophon

Title:	ISO/IEC 20000, A Pocket Guide
Editors:	Jan van Bon (itSMF-NL, chief editor on behalf of itSMF International) Marianne Nugteren (Inform-IT, NL, editor) Selma Polter (Inform-IT, NL, editor)
Publisher:	Van Haren Publishing (info@vanharen.net)
ISBN (13):	978 90 77212 79 0
Edition:	First edition, first impression, May 2006 First edition, second impression, July 2006 First edition, third impression, September 2006 First edition, fourth impression, August 2007 (This is a new edition of a title previously published as BS15000 A Pocket Guide ISBN: 9077212485)

Design & Layout: CO2 Premedia, Amersfoort-NL

Acknowledgement

This pocket guide is an initiative of itSMF, the IT Service Management Forum. In 2004, the Dutch chapter started a project to develop a promotional publicaton, to stimulate the awareness of the BS 15000 standard and provide a quick reference guide. The project was set up with the help of the international itSMF community: it was the first itSMF publication that was produced with the cooperation of all chapters. The IPESC, itSMF International's Publication Executive Sub-Committee has contributed to put together the Review team through its network of subject matter experts, and has continuously discussed progress, tackling all issues that came along with this international project.

This Review Team also reviewed the text of this pocket guide when it was updated to reflect the evolution of BS 15000 into ISO/IEC 20000, to make sure it offers the required high quality entry into the field of ISO/IEC 20000.

The following experts contributed to the Review Team:
    Rolf Akker (Atos Origin, the Netherlands)
    Simon Bos (Bos+Cohen, the Netherlands)
    Bernd Broksch (Siemens Business Services GmbH & Co. OHG, itSMF Germany)
    Janaki Chakravarthy (Infosys, itSMF India)
    Young-Sug Choi (BSI, itSMF Korea)
    Rod Crowder (OpsCentre, Australia)
    Karen Ferris (ProActive Services Pty Ltd, itSMF Australia)
    Marcus Giese (TÜV Informatik Service und Consulting Services GmbH, itSMF Germany)
    Björn Hinrichs (SITGATE AG, itSMF Germany)
    Brian Johnson (Computer Associates, USA)
    Ivor Macfarlane (Guillemot Rock, itSMF International)

Steve Mann (Opsys-SM2, itSMF Belgium)
Colin Rudd (ITEMS Ltd, itSMF UK)
Cheryl E. Simpson (Toronto, Canada)
Wilfred Wah (IBM, itSMF Hong Kong)

We are grateful to these experts, who willingly spent so much of their time on the creation of this pocket guide.

Foreword

The advent of ISO/IEC 20000, which was derived from the British Standard BS 15000, is a testament to the success and popularity of IT Service Management best practices around the world. The recognition of a formal standard helps motivate the service industry further toward service excellence and the means to measure and certify its achievements.

This pocket guide condenses the principles and standards of ISO/IEC 20000 in a manner that helps nurture a basic understanding of the standard, and to serve as a reference to any service provider interested in learning more or perhaps achieving ISO/IEC 20000 certification.

The International itSMF, through the efforts of its International Publications ESC, is proud to endorse this pocket guide as part of a common global library supporting a uniform understanding of ITSM knowledge and best practice.

The colophon on the preceding pages identifies the many itSMF chapter representatives who were involved in the review and endorsement of this book.

On behalf of the itSMF global community I wish to thank the IPESC for their continued dedication, effort and commitment in the review and endorsement of this book.

I trust you will find this book informative and enjoyable.

Sharon Taylor,
Chair, International Publications Executive Sub-Committee
itSMF International

Introduction to the pocket guide

The goal of this publication is to provide an easy to read document that explains the nature, content and aim of ISO/IEC 20000. It should bring ISO/IEC 20000 within reach of a vast international audience at a higher speed, by providing an easy accessible pocket guide:

- to promote the **awareness** and the **acceptability** of ISO/IEC 20000 as a valid standard for IT Service providers;
- to support ISO/IEC 20000 training and certification;
- to produce a **quick reference** to the core content of ISO/IEC 20000, for practitioners.

"ISO/IEC 20000, A Pocket Guide" is aimed at a broad range of practitioners, trainers and students, who work in IT as well as in other environments, ranging from experts in (IT) service provision, to those who are looking for a suitable approach to quality improvement issues. In addition, for customers considering requesting their service providers to become ISO/IEC 20000 certified, they can get an insight into what they can expect from their service providers.

The pocket guide starts with an **Introduction to ISO/IEC 20000**. This covers the history, the background, the position and the environment of ISO/IEC 20000.

The second chapter describes the formal **Structure of the ISO/IEC 20000 standard**. This chapter shows you exactly what you should read if you want to go through the details of the standard in the official documents.

Next is a chapter on **ISO/IEC 20000 - Overall Management**. Here we show you how you can use the standard in a continuous quality improvement approach.

Before going into details of the formal standard we present the **IT Service Management Self-assessment Workbook**. ISO/IEC 20000 is meant to set a specific standard for service providers, which will serve as a target in quality improvement projects. The standard will also be used for assessing the actual position of a service provider. Before you read the details of the standard, you should be aware of the structure of the assessment methodology.

The next chapter is the body of this pocket guide: **ISO/IEC 20000 - Model and Focus Areas**. Here we present the core of the standard, illustrated with example assessment questions.

ISO/IEC 20000 emphasizes the role of communication in service management. For that reason we have added an Appendix with the **Terminology and Definitions** that are used in the standard.

This way all important elements of ISO/IEC 20000 are brought together in a small and handy quick reference guide, which should support rganizations in understanding and applying the standard in their organization.
The pocket guide does not replace the standard: for all details you should read the official ISO documents.

Contents

1 Introduction to ISO/IEC 20000

1.1 History

The IT Infrastructure Library (ITIL) is accepted all over the world as a *de facto* reference for best practice processes in IT Service Management. It wasn't until a few years ago that service providers applying the ITIL framework were able to show their compliance, when a formally documented standard became available. In 2000, BSI, the British Standards Institution, officially determined the requirements for the effective delivery of services to the business and its customers, in a British Standard: BS 15000.

The first edition of BS 15000 was published in November 2000, based on an earlier publication - DISC PD0005:1998 - the Code of Practice for IT Service Management. BS 15000-1:2002 became the second edition, which was the result of experience and feedback from early adopters of the first edition. The development of a certification strategy has given a big impulse to the acceptance of BS 15000 as a formal standard.

On 15 December 2005 ISO, the International Organization for Standardization, accepted BS 15000 as a new international ISO standard: ISO/IEC 20000. There are two ways to create an ISO standard: co-operative creation by involved countries, or the fast-track route based upon a national standard. For the acceptation of this British Standard ISO followed the fast-track route. Preceding the acceptation as an ISO standard BS 15000 was already copied and accepted in the national standards bodies of Australia and South-Africa. The acceptance of ISO/IEC 20000 will freeze its content for three years.

Although ISO/IEC 20000 is not formally including the ITIL approach, it describes an integrated set of management processes that are aligned with and complementary to the process approach defined within ITIL. The individual ITIL books offer expanded information and guidance on the subjects addressed within the scope of ISO/IEC 20000.

The current edition of the *formal specifications* (ISO/IEC 20000-1) is a slightly adapted version of BS 15000-1. The BS 15000 *Code of Practice* (BS 15000-2) had been upgraded to ISO/IEC 20000-2 (Code of Practice). The Code of Practice gives a description of best practices in more detail, and provides guidance and recommendations. This Code of Practice is not part of the requirements.

The transition period for BS 15000 certified organizations to get an ISO/IEC 20000 certificate is 18 months from the publication date of the standard. So after 15 June 2007 certificates issued to BS 15000:2002 part 1 will no longer be valid.

The standard is supported by a practical IT Service Management Self-assessment Workbook (BIP 0015). This publication is an updated version of *the Self-assessment Workbo*ok (PD0015) that was written for BS 15000.

1.2 Changes to the original BS 15000 text

The upgrade to the ISO/IEC 20000 standard caused only minor changes to the original text of BS 15000. Most of these changes were cosmetic and too small to influence the high-level summary of the standard in this pocket guide. The changes that had effect on the first edition of this pocket guide were the following:
• The term 'BS 15000' was replaced with 'ISO/IEC 20000' throughout the book.
• The term 'service organization' was replaced with 'service provider'.
• The term 'third party' was replaced with 'supplier' or 'external'.
• The definitions of 'document' and 'record' were adapted to reflect ISO terminology.

Apart from that, this pocket guide contains some additional text fragments on the certification and accreditation procedures of ISO/IEC 20000.

1.3 The purpose of ISO/IEC 20000

The BS 15000 standard was originally developed by BSI's IT Service Management committee (BDD/3), using a team of industry experts representing a body of knowledge from a wide range of organizations.

The aim of ISO/IEC 20000 - inherited from BS 15000 - is to "provide a common reference standard for any enterprise offering IT services to internal or external customers". Since communication plays an essential role in service management, one of the most important targets of the standard is to create a common terminology for service providers, their suppliers and their customers.

The standard promotes the adoption of an integrated process approach for the management of IT services. These processes have been positioned in a process model, covering the ITIL Service Support and Service Delivery processes, as well as some additional management processes. It sets out to address everything mandatory for good service management - things that are common to and required by every service management service provider - it does not address local requirements directly.

By collating the core information of the ITIL service management processes in an international formalized standard, BSI and now ISO have enabled service providers to determine formal compliancy to these best practices. Until BS 15000 was created the formal certification was focused at *individuals* (ITIL Foundation, ITIL Service Manager, ITIL Practitioner), not at *organizations*. The development of an international organization-focused certificate will stimulate further acceptance of IT service management as an important field.

1.4 Relation to ITIL

As BS 15000 had been aligned to the IT Infrastructure Library (ITIL) Framework defined in the Service Support (2000) and Service Delivery (2001) volumes, ISO/IEC 20000 still is. ITIL is a set of best practices, while ISO/IEC 20000 is a formal set of specifications that a service provider should aim for - to be able to provide high quality services. Applying IT Infrastructure Library best practices will assist a service provider in achieving the quality of service management required by ISO/IEC 20000. BS 15000 and ITIL and now ISO/IEC 20000 have evolved together, with many common contributors.

The relationship between ISO/IEC 20000 and ITIL is illustrated in figure 1.

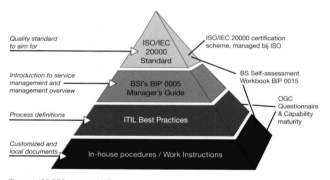

Figure 1. ISO/IEC 20000 and ITIL

ISO/IEC 20000 covers all the explicit ITIL processes from the Service Support and Service Delivery books and Security Management, and also some additional processes which are only partly covered in current ITIL publications. Table 1 illustrates this.

Processes in ISO/IEC 20000	Processes or books in ITIL
Configuration management	Configuration management
Change management	Change management
Release management	Release management
Incident management	Incident management
Problem management	Problem management
Capacity management	Capacity management
Service continuity management and availability management	Service continuity management + Availability management
Service level management	Service level management
Service reporting	-
Information security management	Security management
Budgeting and accounting for IT services	Financial management
Business relationship management	The Business Perspective series and the version one Customer Liaison volume
Supplier management	Version one ITIL books (e.g. managing facilities and third party relationships) and some content in the Business Perspectives book
-	ICT infrastructure management
-	Application management
-	Planning to implement service management

Table 1. Cross reference between processes in ISO/IEC 20000 and ITIL

1.5 Relation to other standards

The current edition of the formal specifications (ISO/IEC 20000) has been adopted with slight adaptations from the BS 15000-1 version. The transition period for current BS 15000 certified organizations to obtain ISO/IEC certification is 18 months from the publication date or 15 June 2007. After this date, certificates issued to BS 15000 Part 1 organizations will no longer be valid.

One of the ISO/IEC 20000 Service Delivery processes is Information security management. ISO/IEC 17799 provides guidance on information security management. Organizations certified to ISO/IEC 27001 will satisfy the security requirements within ISO/IEC 20000-1.

1.6 Stakeholders

British Standards Institution (BSI) are the formal owners of BS 15000. Many international professional bodies were stakeholders in BS 15000:

• The IT Service Management Forum in the UK (itSMF-UK) was administering the formal certification.
• The British Computer Society (BCS) was involved in the BSI team that developed BS 15000.
• The Office of Government Commerce (OGC) was also involved in the BSI development team, and is the owner of ITIL - which made BS 15000 very important for OGC as a supporting structure for ITIL. BS 15000 was highly relevant for OGC as a means to their policy to require the use of standards as a prerequisite for working for UK government in a particular area.
• International stakeholders in relevant countries where the standard had been adopted.

The UK itSMF chapter published a Transition Statement that explains how the validity of BS 15000 certifications will end ultimately within 18 months after the official publication of ISO/IEC 20000. This means that after 15th June 2007, BS 15000 certificates will cease having validity.

Different from BS 15000, ISO/IEC 20000 is managed by the International Organization for Standardization (ISO). ISO is a network of the national standards institutes of 156 countries, on the basis of one member per country, with a Central Secretariat in Geneva, Switzerland, that coordinates the system. ISO is the world's largest developer of standards.

1.7 Accreditation and Certification

Organizations can be assessed for conformity with ISO/IEC 20000 and - if the assessment was positive - they can be certified by official Certification Bodies. Certification bodies need to get accreditation from an Accreditation Organization in a country that is a member of ISO.

The ISO/IEC 20000 standard follows standardized international rules, according to ISO. All countries that are a member of the ISO organization have their own national accreditation bodies, and these accreditation bodies have the invested power to grant certification bodies the right to certify organizations against ISO 20000.

The itSMF Transition Statement explains how certification bodies that want to act under the *British arrangement* will have to register with itSMF-UK, in a cooperation arrangement with the United Kingdom Accreditation Service (UKAS). Certification bodies in other ISO countries can arrange an accreditation with their own, local accreditation organization. Once officially accredited to assess and certify companies against ISO/IEC 20000, they can offer their services anywhere in the market, including the UK, according to standard ISO policies.

The accreditation that itSMF-UK had in place for Course Providers is not applicable to Course providers of ISO/IEC 20000.

The publication of the international ISO/IEC 20000 standard illustrates a step ahead in the global acceptance of ITIL as common best practice, accepted – and managed - by a global community. It is expected that this certification will soon become a default requirement in many contractual arrangements, specifically in larger outsourcing deals.

Apart from professional bodies there is a huge field of service providers, auditors, government & non-commercial organizations, that have an interest in the availability of a widely accepted standard for organizational quality.

1.8 Training

In 2004, itSMF-UK, the owners of the certification scheme for BS 15000, initiated a series of BS 15000 training courses. These courses have since been adapted to ISO/IEC 20000. To date, many organizations around the world offer ISO/IEC 20000 training courses, further demonstrating the wide initial interest in ISO/IEC 20000.

1.9 Certification

Although services providers can claim their compliance with the specifications of the ISO/IEC 20000 standard, a formal audit and certification will carry significantly more weight.

- Service providers that want be certified against the ISO/IEC 20000 standard can contact one of the Registered Certification Bodies (RCBs) anywhere in the world, and apply for certification.
- RCBs are assessed and approved by the certification scheme owner. RCBs will be screened thoroughly for independency and competence. RCB applications are accepted only when coming from Certification Bodies who are accredited by their relevant national accreditation body. Note that an RCB cannot be a company providing ITIL consultancy services because of the conflict of interest; an audit must be independent hence the need to separate audit from consultancy services. The list of accredited RCBs is available from the scheme owner.
- The RCBs will certify IT service providers against the requirements of the standard and issue a certificate.
- Certified service providers are permitted to use the official logo, in accordance with specified restrictions and requirements, and are listed at a public web page.
- Certified service providers will be re-assessed on a regular basis to confirm their compliance to ISO/IEC 20000.

You can find additional information on the procedure, the RCBs, the certified service providers, and the latest news on ISO/IEC 20000 certification via www.bs15000certification.com.

Figure 2. The ISO/IEC 20000 certification logo

2 Structure of the ISO/IEC 20000 standard

2.1 Core material

ISO/IEC 20000 standard is composed of two parts, under the general title **Information Technology - Service Management**:

- **Part 1: Specification** (the Standard); published as ISO/IEC 20000-1: 2005. This is the formal specification of the standard.
- **Part 2: Code of practice**; published as ISO/IEC 20000-2: 2005. This describes best practices in more detail, and provides guidance and recommendations for the service management processes within the scope of the formal standard.

In general, Part 1 of the standard contains a list of mandatory controls, "shalls", that service providers must comply with, in order to be certified. Whereas Part 2 contains a list of guidelines and suggestions that "should" be addressed by service providers wishing to be certified.

> To make clear which parts of this pocket guide text refer to Part I (the "shalls") and which refer to Part II (the "shoulds"), the text of Part I text has been formatted differently.
> This is the format that is used for the prescriptive text originating from Part I.

2.2 Supporting material

ISO/IEC 20000 may also be used in conjunction with the following BSI publication:

- **IT Service Management Self-assessment Workbook**; published as BIP 0015. The Self-assessment Workbook is a checklist that complements this specification. This Workbook has been designed to assist organizations to assess the extent to which their IT services conform to the specified requirements.

At www.bsi-global.com there are more books related to ISO/IEC 20000.

3 ISO/IEC 20000 – Overall management

Using ISO/IEC 20000 requires a well-balanced approach, using management techniques, policies and other management instruments.

To illustrate how the Self-assessment Workbook (BIP 0015) addresses all the requirements of the ISO/IEC 20000 standard, an example question from the workbook is added to relevant paragraphs.

3.1 Scope

In today's business the need to demonstrate the ability to provide services that meet customer requirements is evident. This can be achieved by standardization of service management processes. The specification as applied in ISO/IEC 20000 represents an industry consensus on quality standards for IT service management processes.

It can be used by service providers to:
- monitor and improve their service quality;
- benchmark their IT management services;
- serve as the basis for an independent assessment which may lead to formal certification;
- demonstrate the ability to provide services that meet customer requirement

Service delivery is defined in a number of closely related service management processes, organized in process groups (figure 3). Considering the variety of specific business needs, a service provider may decide that additional objectives and controls are necessary.

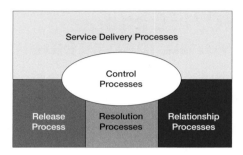

Figure 3. Service management process groups

3.2 Communication

One of the most important issues in managing organizational change is communication. First of all we need to have a common language. This is covered by the reference ISO/IEC 20000 makes towards ITIL and the ITIL terminology and definitions. Secondly we need to see sufficient attention for communication in the procedures and policies of the organization. This is covered in the detailed requirements of the standard.

The core terminology that is used in this pocket guide is listed in an appendix.

3.3 Requirements for a management system

Objective: To provide a management system, including policies and a framework to enable the effective management and implementation of all IT services.

Even if processes are well defined, a systematic approach of IT services is needed to meet the standard. Management shall be well aware of their responsibilities to facilitate the framework needed to implement and maintain IT services. The role of management and their responsibilities shall be clear, and proper documentation shall be guaranteed.

Management responsibilities

Management shall:

• establish the service management policy, objectives and plans;
• communicate the importance of meeting the service management objectives and the need for continual improvement:
• ensure that customer requirements are determined and are met, with the aim of improving customer satisfaction;
• appoint a member of management responsible for the co-ordination and management of all services;
• determine and provide resources to plan, implement, monitor, review and improve service delivery and management e.g. recruit appropriate staff, manage staff turnover;
• manage risks to the service management organization and services;
• conduct reviews of service management, at planned intervals, to ensure continuing suitability, adequacy and effectiveness.

To ensure commitment an owner at senior level should be identified as being responsible and accountable for the service management plan, and for the delivery of the plan. This senior owner should be supported by a decision-taking group with sufficient authority.

Example assessment question:
• *Do individuals, appointed by service management and customers, have the appropriate authority to properly represent their respective organizations?*

Documentation requirements

Service providers shall provide documentation and records to support the management processes such as effective planning, operation and control, including:

• policies and plans;
• Service Level Agreements (SLAs);
• procedures and processes;
• records required by ISO/IEC 20000.

Procedures and responsibilities shall be established for the creation, review, approval, maintenance, disposal and control of documents and records.

The senior responsible owner should ensure that evidence is available for an audit of service management policies, plans and procedures.

There should be a process for the creation and management of documents and documentation should be protected from damage.

> Example assessment question:
> • *Is there a published policy on service improvement?*

Competence, awareness and training

Staff shall be aware of the relevance and importance of their activities within the wider business context and how they contribute to the achievement of quality objectives. To ensure that service management staff is competent, the required competence for each role shall be determined.

A training plan should ensure that requirements for new or expanded services are met.

> Example assessment question:
> • *Are staff competencies and training needs reviewed and managed such that the staff can deliver their responsibilities effectively?*

3.4 Planning and implementing service management

In planning and implementing service management a range of processes, decisions and responsibilities are to be dealt with. Questions that will rise are: what are customer requirements; which business processes are to be supported; who will perform which activity and when; what are the financial and infrastructural resources available; when are objectives met.

In order to analyze this information and monitor progress in the field of IT service processes, Deming's Quality Circle (PDCA: Plan-Do-Check-Act) can be applied (figure 4).

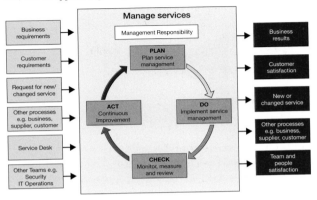

Figure 4. Plan-Do-Check-Act methodology for service management processes (Deming's Quality Circle)

The model assumes that to provide appropriate quality, the following steps must be undertaken repeatedly:

- **Plan** - establish the objectives and processes necessary to deliver the results. This stage is completed with agreements that are measurable and realistic, and a plan of how they are to be achieved.
- **Do** - implement the processes.
- **Check** - monitor and measure processes and services against policies, objectives and requirements.
- **Act** - identify actions to continually improve performance.

By going through this cycle again and again, a step-by-step quality improvement can be assured. This is known as the 'uphill cycle of never-ending improvement' (figure 5).

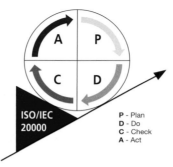

P - Plan
D - Do
C - Check
A - Act

Figure 5. Deming's PDCA quality improvement cycle

Documentation is very important in successful application of the PDCA model. As the output of each activity is the input of the next activity in the model, a constant feedback is realized and transparency in relationships between processes is created.

 Plan service management (PLAN)
Objective: To plan the implementation and delivery of service management.

Planning is the part of the process where management provides direction and documented responsibilities. Service management planning should translate customer requirements into tangible service targets, providing a route map for directing progress.

The overall Service Management Plan shall at a minimum define:
• the scope of the service provider's service management (this should be checked for suitability under ISO/IEC 20000-1);
• the objectives to be achieved;
• processes to be executed; examples are: implementation, delivery, changes and improvement of service management processes.
• management roles and responsibilities;
• translation of the service management processes into activities;

- the approach of identifying, assessing and managing issues and risks;
- resources, facilities and budget;
- methods to manage, audit and improve the quality of the service.

All plans shall be reviewed, authorized and communicated. Any process specific plans shall be compatible with the Service Management Plan.

> Example assessment question:
> - *Is there clear management direction and documented responsibility for reviewing, authorizing, communicating, implementing and maintaining the service management plan?*

 ## Implement service management and provide the services (DO)
Objective: To implement the service management objectives and plan.

The Service Management Plan shall be implemented by the following actions:
- allocation of budgets, roles and responsibilities;
- managing budgets and facilities;
- co-ordination of service management processes;
- recruiting and developing staff and staff continuity;
- managing teams, including service desk and operations;
- documenting and maintaining plans and policies, procedures and definitions for each process;
- reporting progress against plans;
- identify and manage risks to the service.

To achieve ISO/IEC 20000 the original service management plan shall explicitly meet the requirements of the standard.

Once implemented, the organization should stay focused at maintaining and improving the processes and the achieved service quality. This may mean that staff responsible for the implementation will be exchanged by suitable other staff, responsible for the ongoing operation.

> Example assessment question:
> • *Are all IT service management policies, plans, procedures and definitions formally documented?*

Monitoring, measuring and reviewing (CHECK)

Objective: To monitor, measure and review that the service management objectives and plan are being achieved.

The service provider shall demonstrate the effectiveness of processes by means of monitoring and measuring. Management shall conduct reviews at planned intervals to determine whether the service management requirements:
• conform with the service management plan and to the requirements of the standard;
• are effectively implemented and maintained.

To conduct reviews, all services should be monitored, measured and analyzed. Items to monitor, measure and analyze are:
• achievements against defined service targets;
• customer satisfaction;
• resource utilization and trends;
• non-conformities.

An audit programme shall be planned, taking into consideration:
• status and importance of the processes;
• definition of criteria, scope, frequency and methods;
• results of previous audits;
• selection of auditors (auditors shall not audit their own work);
• communication of results to relevant parties;
• identification of significant areas of noncompliance.

The results of reviews and audits provide input to the next step in the PDCA cycle: act to improve service processes.

Continual improvement (ACT)

Objective: To improve the effectiveness and efficiency of service delivery and management.

A published policy is required, with clear definitions of roles and responsibilities for service improvement activities. Any non-compliance with the service management plans shall be remedied. A service improvement plan shall be used to handle all suggested service improvements. A specific process is required for handling the service improvements.

The service improvement plan and process shall cover:
- relevant inputs about improvement and set targets;
- how to identify, plan, communicate and implement improvement;
- how to measure, report and communicate the improvements;
- how to revise service management policies, plans, processes and procedures where necessary;
- how to ensure that all approved actions are delivered and that they achieve their intended objectives.

Improvements concerning individual processes can be managed by the process owner. Major service improvements, e.g. improvements across the organization or across more than one process, shall be managed as a project or as several projects.

Before implementing a service improvement plan, service quality and levels shall be recorded as a baseline against which the actual improvements can be compared.

The actual improvement should be compared to the predicted improvement to assess the effectiveness of the change.

Service management staff should be very aware of the service quality policy, the processes, and their own contribution to this. This policy is based on the perception that there are always opportunities to make delivery of services more effective and efficient.

> Example assessment question:
> • *Does the operation of the Service Management Programme demonstrate evidence of continuous improvement in service quality?*

3.5 Planning and implementing new or changed services

Objective: To ensure that new services and changes to services will be deliverable and manageable at the agreed cost and service quality.

Any new or changed service shall be planned and implemented according to procedures described in the previous section. The cost, organizational, technical and commercial impact of any proposed new or changed service shall be considered, including a thorough impact analysis.

New or changed services, including closure of a service, shall be planned and implemented through formal change management. The plans need to cover:
• roles and responsibilities for implementing, operating and maintaining the new or changed service;

- changes to the existing service management framework and services;
- communication to the relevant parties;
- new or changed contracts and agreements to align with the changes in business need;
- manpower and recruitment requirements;
- skills and training requirements, e.g. users, technical support;
- processes, measures, methods and tools to be used in connection with the new or changed service;
- budgets and time-scales;
- service acceptance criteria;
- the expected outcomes from operating the new service expressed in measurable terms.

All service changes should be reflected in Change Management records.

Example assessment question:
- *Are proposals for new or significantly changed services considered in terms of the potential cost, organizational, technical and commercial impact?*

4 Self-assessment Workbook

Before explaining the details of the various service management processes the role of the related IT Service Management Self-assessment Workbook will be described. This Workbook provides a very useful resource to translate the abstract requirements of the standard into practical terms. In the previous chapters some example questions were shown to illustrate this. Similar example questions will be used throughout the rest of this pocket guide.

The Self-assessment Workbook reflects the requirements detailed in ISO/IEC 20000-1: 2005 and can be used by service providers to:

• compare their IT service management processes with those described in ISO/IEC 20000-1: 2005;
• check if the major areas of service management are addressed;
• identify where resources should be concentrated for the best return in terms of process improvement;
• identify the most effective use of consultancy;
• review the implementation of accepted best practice for IT service management processes;
• support internal and external reviews.

4.1 Structure

The Self-assessment Workbook comprises a general part concerning IT service management and high-level service management processes, and questionnaires on each of the individual processes. The IT service management and high-level process assessment, referred to as High Level Concerns, is an overview section. Prior to any individual process assessment it is recommended that the High Level Concerns are addressed. Service management does not function effectively without the presence of efficient high level and general service management processes.

Each process section contains questions that are grouped under the following headings:
• process overview;
• process scope;
• activities;
• control, reporting and auditing.

To give you an idea of what the self-assessment looks like, an example of a page of the Self-assessment Workbook is shown in figure 6.

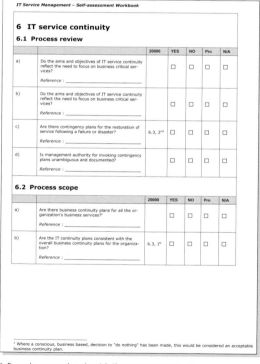

Figure 6. Example page or the related Self-assessment Workbook

ISO/IEC 20000 - A Pocket Guide

4.2 How to use the Workbook

Each Question can be answered in one of four ways: [**Yes**], [**No**], [**Pro**] (=in progress) or [**N/A**] (not applicable). The questions should be answered accurately and as objectively as possible. To ensure a more credible assessment, it is best not to let staff review their own processes, or to make sure that answers are peer-reviewed.

Most questions reference explicitly the paragraph within the ISO/IEC 20000-1: 2005, to which they refer. Although there are questions that do not map directly to the text, it is essential that they are not skipped. They too relate directly to processes that support the requirements of the standard.

At the end of each question, in the [*Reference*] field, there is room for some 'proof' of the answer given. Here a user can refer to a specific document in the assessed organization, or to well-known local situations. These references can be used to follow-up on the assessed matter.

Based on the results of a self-assessment, service providers can analyze their situation in more detail, organize workshops to discuss matters that should be improved, or build specific improvement programmes. By repeating the assessment at regular intervals, service providers should be able to demonstrate service improvement.

To illustrate how the Self-assessment Workbook can be applied in practice, examples of self-assessment questions are shown in each paragraph of the next chapter.

5 ISO/IEC 20000 - Model and Focus Areas

After describing the more general aspects of ISO/IEC 20000 in chapter 3, and the supporting Workbook in chapter 4, we now show the processes of ISO/IEC 20000 in more detail. Using the overall management approach and the Self-assessment Workbook one should be able to apply one, more or all of these processes in a quality improvement approach.

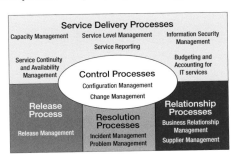

Figure 7. Service management processes

5.1 Service Delivery processes

Service delivery includes the processes that negotiate, define and agree the actual service levels, and that report performance against targets.

As illustrated in figure 7 the following processes are part of the service delivery domain:
- Service Level Management
- Service Reporting
- Capacity Management
- Service Continuity and Availability Management
- Information Security Management
- Budgeting and Accounting for IT Services

Service Level Management (SLM)

Objective: To define, agree, record and manage levels of service.

The full range of services shall be agreed and documented. Each service to be delivered shall be recorded in an SLA together with the corresponding targets. Supporting agreements, supplier contracts and corresponding procedures shall also be agreed by all relevant parties and recorded. To keep SLAs up-to-date they shall be reviewed by the relevant parties and maintained under the control of the change management process.

To enhance quality, service levels shall be monitored and reported against targets. Any non-conformance shall be reported and reviewed and provides input to plans for improving the service.

IT service providers should produce a service catalogue showing the full range of services available to their customers. The catalogue is a key document for setting customer expectations and should be easily accessible to both customers and support staff.

The SLA's are formally authorized by representatives of the customer and the service provider. The content of the SLA should be based on the customers' business needs and their budget. Targets, against which the delivered services are to be measured, should be defined from a customer perspective. An SLA is a non-technical document.
Business changes, due to growth or reorganization or otherwise, can require the adjustment of service levels.

The minimum content of an SLA should be:
• Description of service, service targets, communications and reporting;
• Authorization details and validity period;
• Financial management details;
• Service provider liability and obligations, e.g security;
• Customer responsibilities, e.g. security;

- Supporting and related services;
- Impact, urgency and priority guidelines;
- Service hours e.g. 7.00h to 18.00 h, date exceptions, critical business periods and out-of-hours cover;
- Workload limits e.g. agreed number of users/volume of work;
- Contact details of people authorized to act in case of emergencies;
- Actions to be taken in the event of a service interruption;
- Escalation and notification process;
- Scheduled and agreed interruptions ;
- Complaints procedures;
- Housekeeping procedures;
- Exceptions to the terms given in the SLA;
- Glossary of terms.

Underpinning operational support services, relevant to SLA's, should to be identified. These underpinning services should to be documented and agreed with each service supplier in either operational level agreements (OLA's: in case of internal suppliers), or in underpinning contracts (UC's: when external suppliers are contracted).

> Example assessment questions:
> - *Is each service defined, agreed and documented in at least one SLA?*
> - *Have all underpinning support services relevant to SLA's been identified?*
> - *Does the SLM process consider the costs of delivering service and business justification of those costs?*

Service Reporting
Objective: To produce agreed, reliable, timely and accurate reports for informed decision making and effective communication.

Each service report shall include its identity, purpose, audience and details of the data source.
Service reporting shall include:

- Performance against service level targets;
- Performance characteristics of each operational process, like workload statistics and resource utilization;
- Performance reporting following major events (major changes, releases);
- Trend information;
- Non compliance and issues, e.g. against the SLA, security breach;
- Satisfaction analyses.

Issues that stem from detailed process reports, like reports on scheduled and future workloads can be included in the service reporting as well. The success of all management processes depends on the use of the information provided in service reports. Service reports are used as a decision support tool. There can be several types of reports: reactive and proactive reports, and scheduled reports showing planned activities. Service monitoring and reporting encompasses all measurable aspects of the service, providing both current and historical analysis.

> Example assessment questions:
> - *Does the IT service management plan clearly identify which service reports are needed and from where the data for these are derived?*
> - *Is an annual report on the Service Improvements Programme targets and results produced and made available to appropriate parties?*

Service Continuity and Availability Management

Objective: To ensure that agreed service continuity and availability commitments to customers can be met in all circumstances.

To meet these objectives availability and service continuity requirements shall be identified on the basis of business plans, SLAs and risk assessments. Requirements shall include access rights and response times as well as end-to-end availability of system components. Availability and service continuity plans shall be developed, tested and maintained to ensure these requirements can be met.

Availability shall be measured and recorded. Any unplanned non-availability shall be investigated and appropriate actions shall be taken. Where possible, potential issues shall be predicted and preventive actions shall be taken.

The overall objective of availability and service continuity management is to control risks and to maintain business continuity in case of lesser (incidents) or bigger events (disasters), e.g. a virus outbreak, a DoS-attack or an earthquake.

All information on availability and service continuity is linked up in the availability and service continuity plans. The plans are:
• reviewed and maintained at least annually;
• communicated to change management in order to determine impact of any change on availability and service continuity;
• tested in accordance with business needs;
• available when normal office access is prevented.

Availability management should:
• monitor and record availability of service components;
• maintain historical data;
• make comparisons with requirements defined in SLA's to identify non-conformance to the agreed availability targets;
• identify, document and review non-conformance;
• predict future availability.

Service continuity management defines:
• maximum acceptable periods of lost service;
• maximum acceptable periods of degraded service;
• recording and maintenance;
• responsibility;
• document, data and software backups for service restoration;
• staff and instruction of staff necessary for service restoration;
• backups of service continuity documents at secure remote locations.

Service continuity management takes into account the dependencies between service and system components. Prior to any system or service change the impact on the service continuity should be determined. Service continuity plans, therefore, should be communicated to the support processes, e.g. to change management.

To assure that continuity plans remain effective in the face of changing systems, processes, personnel and business needs, frequent testing is of the utmost importance. All parties, i.e. customer and service providers, should be involved in the testing. Test results are documented and reviewed to be used for service improvement.

Example assessment questions:
- *Do the aims and objectives of availability management reflect the need to focus on business critical services?*
- *Are the reasons for non-conformance to agreed service availability, as identified by the service provider, identified and documented, and is appropriate action taken?*
- *Is the availability plan reviewed at least annually to ensure that requirements are being met?*
- *Are reports produced on tests of the continuity plans?*

Budgeting and Accounting for IT Services
Objective: To budget and account for the cost of service provision.

There shall be clear policies and processes for:
- budgeting and accounting for all components including IT assets, shared resources, overheads, externally supplied services, people, insurance and licenses;
- apportioning indirect costs and allocating direct costs to services;
- financial control and authorization.

Costs shall be budgeted in sufficient detail to enable effective financial

control and decision making. The service provider shall:
• monitor and report costs against budget;
• review the financial forecasts;
• manage costs accordingly.

Note: The actual accounting practices in IT have to be aligned with the wider accountancy practices of the service provider. Charging is not covered by ISO/IEC 20000, since charging is an optional activity.

Budgeting and accounting for IT services is focused at the practices to be carried out in order to meet the requirements of ISO/IEC 20000. Responsibility for financial decisions will normally lie outside the scope of the service management. Requirements for what financial information should be provided is most probably dictated from outside.

Accounting processes are recording the use of financial resources, which enables the determination of costs per user, per unit or per activity. Accounting reports can be used to make cost effectiveness comparisons and to build cost models, for financial management to act upon.

The policy on financial management may define:
• the objectives to be met by budgeting and accounting;
• the level of detail, e.g. cost types apportionment of overhead costs;
• the level of charging detail;
• cost tracking against budget to provide early warning of variance;
• cost models to demonstrate the costs of service provision;
• manner of handling variances against budgets.

The level of investment in budgeting and accounting is based on the needs of the customer and the service provider. Operating in a commercial environment, a service provider might need much more detailed financial management information than when working in an organization where simple identification of costs is sufficient.

Capacity Management

Objective: To ensure that the service provider has, at all times, sufficient capacity to meet the current and future agreed demands of customer's business needs.

Capacity management shall produce and maintain a capacity plan which addresses the business needs. Capacity management shall identify and apply methods, procedures and techniques in order to monitor, tune and provide adequate service capacity. Furthermore, capacity management shall address changes in the required infrastructure, ranging from variations in business requirements and the effects of new technologies, to the impact of external changes.

Capacity management should supply sufficient capacity for storage and processing of data and should be cost-efficient. To keep the capacity plan up-to-date, it is evaluated and adjusted annually. Effects of service upgrades, requests for change, new technologies and techniques, and external changes should be evaluated and 'included' in the capacity plan.

This should assure achievement of the agreed service level targets as defined in the SLA.
In order to determine the required capacity, business predictions and workload estimates should be translated into specific requirements.

Information Security Management

Objective: To manage information security effectively within all service activities.

Note: ISO/IEC 17799, Information technology - Security techniques - Code of practice for information security management, provides guidance on information security management, whereas ISO/IEC 27001 specifies the requirements for a documented Information Security Management System.

Management with appropriate authority shall approve an information security policy that shall be communicated to all relevant parties. Security controls shall operate to:
• implement the requirements of the information security policy;
• manage risks associated with access to the service or systems.

Security controls shall be documented, describing:
• risks to which the controls relate;
• manner of operation and maintenance of the controls;
• relation to implemented changes.

There shall be procedures to ensure that:
• security incidents are reported and recorded in line with incident management procedures;
• all security incidents are investigated and management action taken;
• types, volumes and impacts of security incidents and malfunctions are monitored by adequate mechanisms;
• external access to systems and services is based on adequate formal agreements.

Information security management protects information and equipment used in connection with its storage, transmission and processing. Information security provides controlled access and prevents abuse of data. Risks are identified and controlled. To achieve this, policies and procedures are designed, to cover all service activities, addressing:

- roles, responsibilities and post holders;
- methods to monitor and maintain the effectiveness of the information security policy;
- assurance of staff competence, awareness and training;
- availability of expert help on risk management and control implementation;
- no compromises on the effectiveness of controls in case of changes;
- co-operation with incident management procedures in handling information security incidents.

Information assets like computers, other means of communication, documents and all other data are:

- categorized according to its criticality to the service;
- inventoried and judged on the level of protection it requires.

On each asset an owner is nominated to be accountable for providing the protection and manage security.

Risks to information assets are assessed with reference to:

- their nature, e.g software malfunction, operating errors or physical damage;
- past experience and likelihood;
- potential business impact, e.g disclosure of sensitive information to unauthorized parties or information being unavailable to use.

Security risk assessment should be performed at agreed intervals and should be recorded. Maintaining risk assessments during changes, like changing business needs, processes or configuration changes, keeps them relevant and up-to-date. It helps to understand the impact of security on managed services, and it supports decision taking in regard to the types of controls to be operated.

Proper recording provides the management with information on:
- effectiveness of security policy and control over access to information, assets and systems;
- emerging trends on security incidents;
- input to service improvement.

Service providers should operate adequate controls to manage information security:
- the security management policy should be communicated to IT staff by senior management;
- roles and responsibilities should be defined and allocated;
- all staff should be aware and well trained on security issues;
- changes need to involve assessment of security aspects;
- information security incidents should be under incident control;
- management information on information security effectiveness and trends should be produced.

Note: Account should also be taken of information security policy objectives, the need to meet the customers' specified security requirements and statutory or regulatory requirements that apply.

Note: ISO/IEC 17799 provides guidance on information security management. Implementation of the requirements of ISO/IEC 20000-1 may not satisfy all the requirements that are necessary to obtain certification against ISO/IEC 27001. Organizations certified to ISO/IEC 27001 will satisfy the security requirements within ISO/IEC 20000-1.

Example assessment questions:
- *Are the information security aims and objectives established via risk management considerations?*
- *Are the contents of the information security policy published and communicated as appropriate to all system users, including service management personnel, customers and suppliers?*

5.2 Relationship processes

Relationship processes describe the two related aspects of supplier management and business relationship management. The service provider fills a role within a supply chain, receiving goods or services from suppliers and delivering a seamless service to the customer (figure 8).

Both supplier and customer can be internal or external to the service provider's organization. External relationships will be formalized via underpinning contracts (UCs); internal relationships will be formalized by service or operational level agreements (SLAs or OLAs).

Relationship processes should ensure that customer satisfaction levels are appropriate and that future business needs are communicated and understood.

To establish and maintain good relationships, connections should to be clear to all parties. They should define and agree on:
• business needs;
• capabilities and constraints;
• scope, roles and responsibilities of the relationships;
• identification of the stakeholders;
• contracts;
• frequency and lines of communication.

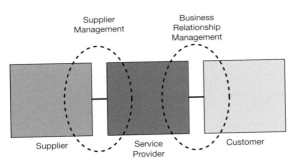

Figure 8. Relationship processes

Business Relationship Management

Objective: To establish and maintain a good relationship between the service provider and the customer based on understanding the customer and their business drivers.

Business relationship management includes service reviews, service complaints and customer satisfaction measurement.

The service provider shall identify and document the stakeholders and customers of the services. The service provider and the customer shall attend reviews at least annually and before and after major changes. The reviews are to consider:
- changes in service scope;
- SLA's and contracts;
- current and projected business needs;
- past performance.

To discuss performance, achievements, issues and action plans, interim meetings are held. All meetings shall be documented. The service provider plans and records all formal meetings, issue records and follows up agreed actions.

The business relationship management process shall document and agree a formal complaints procedure with its customers. Records of complaints shall be analyzed periodically and the complaints procedure shall include:

• handling of complaints, i.e. record, investigate, act upon;
• reporting and formal closure of all complaints;
• a procedure for escalation of outstanding complaints.

The service provider shall have a named individual who is responsible for managing customer satisfaction and the business relationship process. A process shall exist for obtaining and acting upon feedback from regular customer satisfaction measurements. Results of feedback and complaints analysis shall be used as input to the service improvement plan.

Customer satisfaction is measured to enable the service provider to compare performance with customer satisfaction targets and previous surveys. Variations in satisfaction levels should be investigated and understood.

Results and conclusions of surveys are discussed with the customer and should lead to service improvement. Compliments about the service should be documented and reported to the service delivery team.

Example assessment questions:
• *Is there a named individual or team responsible for managing the process?*
• *Has it been agreed with the customer what constitutes a formal complaint?*
• *Are there customer satisfaction measurements at an appropriate frequency?*

Supplier management

Objective: To manage third party suppliers to ensure the provision of seamless, quality services.

In most cases there will be several suppliers, sometimes divided in lead and subcontracted suppliers (figure 9). In order to tune suppliers and internal services, the service provider is charged with managing the relationships, (underpinning) contracts and deliverable services. The service provider has documented supplier management processes and shall appoint a contract manager responsible for the relationship with each supplier.

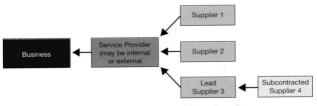

Figure 9. Example of relationship between service providers and suppliers

For each service and supplier the service provider shall maintain:
- a definition of services, scope, roles and responsibilities documented in SLA's or other documents;
- alignment of supplier contracts with the business SLA's;
- clearly documented roles and relationships between lead and subcontracted suppliers;
- review of contracts and changes to the contract and SLA's;
- a process to deal with contractual disputes, expected and unexpected end of the service;
- monitoring and reviewing and recording performance against service level targets;
- a formal process to deal with contractual disputes;
- contract (SLA) changes in line with change management process.

Performance against service level targets shall be monitored and reviewed. Actions for improvement identified during this process shall be recorded and input into the service improvement plan.

It shall be clear whether the service provider is dealing with all suppliers directly or a lead supplier is taking responsibility for subcontract suppliers. The service provider shall obtain evidence that lead suppliers are formally managing subcontracted suppliers guided by the requirements of ISO/IEC 20000-1.

Processes referring to contractual disputes are defined in the contract. This includes an escalation route. The process should ensure that disputes are recorded, investigated, acted upon and formally closed. Contracts also define an end-of-contract situation - either expected or early end - and provide for the transfer of the service to another party.

> Example assessment questions:
> * *Is a named contract manager responsible for each supplier?*
> * *Are roles and relationships between lead and subcontracted suppliers clearly documented?*

5.3 Resolution processes

The resolution processes incident and problem management are separate processes, although they are closely linked. Incident management deals with the restoration of services to users whereas problem management identifies and removes the causes of incidents.

Where appropriate, problem management develops workarounds to enable incident management to restore service and to minimize the impact on the customer's business activities.

Incident Management

Objective: To restore agreed service to the business as soon as possible or to respond to service requests.

To restore agreed service as soon as possible procedures shall be adopted to manage the impact of service incidents. All incidents shall be recorded and procedures shall define the:
* business impact;
* recording and prioritization;

- classification, updating, escalation;
- resolution and formal closure.

Major incidents shall be classified and managed according to a defined process.

Incident management shall keep the customer informed of the progress of their reported incident or service request and alerted in advance if their service levels cannot be met.

All staff involved in incident management shall have access to relevant information such as known errors, problem resolutions and the configuration management database (CMDB).

Incidents are reported by users or relevant IT staff at the service desk and recorded in a manner that allows relevant information to be retrieved and analyzed. Incidents can also be produced by automated detection mechanisms based on monitoring tools. Incident management staff have access to an up-to-date knowledge base. This data base holds information on technical specialists, previous incidents and resolutions, related problems and known errors that will help restoring service as soon as possible. The scheduling of incident resolution takes into account:
- priority based on impact and urgency;
- skills available;
- communication to users about status of incidents;
- resolution (providing service continuity);
- escalation if necessary;
- updating and formal closure of incident record.

There should be a clear definition of what constitutes a major incident and who is empowered to invoke changes to the normal operation of the incident/problem process. A major incident should have a clearly defined responsible manager who coordinates and controls all aspects for the resolution. This includes escalation and communication across all areas involved in the resolution.

Problem Management

Objective: To minimize disruption to the business by proactive identification and analysis of the cause of incidents and by managing problems to closure.

Problem management proactively prevents the recurrence or replication of incidents or known errors.

Procedures shall be adopted to identify, minimize or avoid the impact of incidents and problems. Those procedures shall define:
• Recording and classification all problems;
• Updating of all problems;
• Escalation, resolution and closure of all problems.

Furthermore managing problems shall include:
• reviewing to reduce problems by prevention, e.g. following trend analysis of incident volumes and types;
• passing required changes to change management;
• monitoring, reviewing and reporting of problem resolutions;
• providing up-to-date information on known errors and corrected problems to incident management;
• providing input to the service improvement plan.

When investigation has identified the root cause of an incident and a method of resolving the incident, the problem is qualified as a known error. Resolving the incident does not imply that the underlying cause has been eliminated. Known errors should not be closed until a successful solution is applied. All known errors are recorded in an up-to-date database to help restore service in a minimum of time. Reviews should be held on unsolved problems, e.g unusual or high-impact problems, and to analyze trends to provide input on other processes such as customer or service desk education.

Incidents and problem records can be closed if the customer agrees that a resolution has been achieved. The record is logged and the cause is categorized.

Proactive problem management leads to a reduction of problems and incidents. Problem prevention can range from prevention of individual incidents, such as repeated difficulties with a particular feature, through to strategic decisions. The latter can require major expenditure to implement, such as investment in a better network. At this level proactive problem management merges into availability management. Problem prevention should also include training of users, preventing incidents caused by a lack of user knowledge.

Example assessment questions:
- *Are staff in problem management responsible for ensuring that a knowledge base of incident information is available and up-to-date?*
- *Are regular management reviews held to highlight problems requiring immediate attention, to determine and analyze trends, and to provide input for other processes such as customer or service desk education?*

5.4 Control processes

Change and configuration management are two core processes in the process model. These processes enable a service provider to control the components of the service and infrastructure, and maintain accurate information on the configuration. This accurate information is a basic requirement for decision making in the change management process, as well as for all other processes in the IT service organization.

Configuration Management

Objective: To define and control the components of the service and infrastructure, and maintain accurate configuration information.

Note: Financial asset accounting falls outside of the scope of configuration management.

There shall be an integrated approach to change and configuration management planning. Configuration management shall provide information to the change management process on the impact of a requested change on the service and infrastructure configurations.

What is defined as a configuration item and its components is documented in a policy. Methods for identifying, controlling and tracking of components is provided by configuration management.

All configuration items shall be uniquely identified and defined to describe their functional and physical characteristics. The information to be recorded for each item shall be defined and shall include the relationships and documentation necessary for effective service management. The configuration management database (CMDB) shall be actively managed and verified to ensure its reliability and accuracy.

Changes to configuration items e.g. changes and movements of software and hardware shall be traceable and auditable.

To protect its integrity the CMDB shall be held in a secure environment which prevents unauthorized access, provides means for disaster recovery and permits the retrieval of copies of the controlled masters, e.g. software and support documents. Configuration control procedures shall ensure that the integrity of systems, services and service components is maintained.

Configuration audit procedures shall include:
• recording deficiencies;

- methods on improvement actions;
- reporting on the outcome

All major assets and configurations should have a responsible manager who ensures appropriate protection and control, e.g. changes are authorized before implementation.

A configuration plan should include:
- scope, objectives, policy, roles and responsibilities;
- definition, recording and reporting of configuration items;
- requirements for accountability, traceability, auditability, e.g. for security or legal or business purposes;
- configuration control, e.g. owner of the configuration item, access, protection, version and release control.

Items that should be registered in the configuration management database (CMDB) include:
- issues and releases of systems and software and related documentation, e.g. requirements specifications, test reports, release documentation and ownership;
- configuration baselines or build statements for applicable environment, standard hardware builds and release;
- master hardcopy and electronic libraries;
- licenses and security components e.g firewalls, secure magnetic media;
- service related documentation, e.g. SLA's;
- service supporting facilities, e.g. power to computer room;
- relationships and dependencies between configuration items.

Configuration information should be kept current and made available for planning, decision making and managing changes to the defined configuration. Configuration management reports should be made available to all relevant parties. Reports should cover latest configuration item versions, location of item, interdependencies and version history.

Verification and audit processes should be scheduled to ensure that the service provider:
- is in control of its configurations, master copies and licenses;
- protects it's physical and intellectual capital;
- provides confidence that configuration information is accurate, controlled and visible;
- provides changes, releases and environments conform to specified requirements.

Configuration audits should be held to check on performance and functional characteristics of specified configuration documents (functional audit) as well as to verify that configuration items conform to their product "as built/produced" specifications (physical audit). Deficiencies and non-conformities should be recorded and fed back to the relevant parties.

> Example assessment questions:
> - *Is there a well understood policy defining what constitutes a configuration item?*
> - *Do procedures prevent configuration records being added, modified, replaced or removed without appropriate authority or controlling documentation?*
> - *Are regular and accurate reports produced for management?*

Change Management

Objective: To ensure all changes are assessed, approved, implemented and reviewed in a controlled manner.

Changes, like new releases, version updates, hardware moves, or changes resulting from incident/problem solutions, do have their impact on the IT service environment. To ensure that all changes are approved, implemented and reviewed in a controlled manner, change management controls the processing of all changes to the infrastructure.

All changes shall be recorded and classified (e.g. urgent, major, minor) and the process shall provide procedures, which include:

- a defined and documented scope for all service and infrastructural changes;
- assessment of changes for risks, impact and business benefits;
- the manner in which unsuccessful changes shall be reversed or remedied;
- policies and procedures for emergency changes;
- change scheduling, monitoring en reporting;
- approval, checking, scheduling and controlling of the implementation of changes;
- a post implementation review.

Change records shall be analyzed regularly to detect increasing levels of changes, frequently recurring change categories, emerging trends and other relevant information.

All changes shall be reviewed for success or failure after implementation. Results of reviews shall be fed into the service improvement plan.

A schedule that contains details of all the changes approved for implementation and their proposed implementation dates shall be maintained and communicated to relevant parties to serve as the basis for change and release scheduling.

Scheduling information should be available to the people affected by the change.

A post-implementation review should be undertaken for major changes to check that:

- the change met its objectives;
- the customers are contented with the results;
- there have been no unexpected side effects.

Deficiencies identified in a review of the change management process should be fed into the plans for improving the service.

> Example assessment questions:
> - *Are there formal procedures to ensure that all changes are approved, checked and implemented in controlled manner?*
> - *Are change records analyzed regularly to detect increasing levels of change, frequently recurring types, emerging trends and other relevant information?*

5.5 Release process

While change management is focused at controlling changes, release management delivers the planned changes. Release management should be integrated with the configuration and change management processes to ensure tuning and settling of releases and executed changes. Release management coordinates the activities of the service provider, suppliers and the business to plan and deliver a release in the IT environment.

Release Management process

Objective: To deliver, distribute and track one or more changes in a release into the live environment.

Note: The release management process should be integrated with the configuration and change management processes.

Good planning and management are essential to successfully distribute a release and to manage the associated impact and risks.

The release policy stating frequency and type of releases shall be documented and agreed.

The release policy should define:
- the roles and responsibilities;
- the authority for releasing versions into acceptance, test and production environments;
- the unique identification, description, verification and acceptance of all releases;

- the approach to grouping changes into a release;
- the approach to automating the build, installation and release distribution processes to aid repeatability and efficiency.

The service provider shall plan the release of services, systems, software and hardware. Plans how to roll out the release shall be agreed and authorized by all relevant parties e.g. customers, users operations and support staff. The roll out plan shall include:
- recording of release date and deliverables;
- references to related change requests, known errors and problems;
- manner in which the release is remedied if unsuccessful;
- communication to incident management

The roll out plan may also define:
- identification of dependencies;
- communication, preparation, documentation and training for customer and support staff;
- verification and acceptance;
- release and sign off;
- scheduling of post-release audits.

All documentation on new releases is according to the requirements of the CMDB. After successful installation the asset and configuration management records shall be updated. Change management shall execute a post-implementation review. Recommendations shall be fed into the service improvement plan.

Release and distribution shall be designed and implemented so that the integrity of hardware and software is maintained during installation, handling, packaging and delivery. A controlled acceptance test environment shall be established to build and test all releases prior to distribution.

Information systems and software releases from in-house teams, system builders or other organizations are verified on receipt.

The release and distribution are designed to:

- conform with the systems architecture, service management and infrastructural standards;
- identify risks, so remedial actions can be taken if required;
- enable verification that the target platform satisfies prerequisites before installation;
- enable verification that a release is complete when it reaches its destination.

The output from this process is used for testing and includes release notes, installation instructions, installed software and hardware with related configuration baseline.

The end result is signed-off on completeness against requirements.

Verification and acceptance processes should:

- verify that the controlled acceptance test environment matches the requirements of target production environments;
- ensure that the release is created from versions under configuration management;
- verify that the testing has been completed, e.g. functional and non-functional tests, business acceptance test, testing of build, release, distribution and installation procedures;
- ensure that the release is tested to the satisfaction of customers and service provider staff;
- ensure that the release authority signs off each stage of acceptance testing;
- verify that the target platform satisfies the hardware and software prerequisites and that a release is complete when it reaches its destination.

Example assessment questions:
- *Are there appropriate and comprehensive plans on how to roll out a release to each site and user agreed and signed off by all potentially affected parties?*
- *Are all releases built and tested in a controlled acceptance test environment before release?*

6 Appendices

6.1 The Certification Scheme

Claims to conform to the requirements of the ISO/IEC 20000 standard can be independently verified as part of a formal certification scheme, managed through ISO. ISO has determined standards for Accreditation Bodies that can accredit Conformity Assessment Bodies (CABs, certification bodies). "Conformity assessment" is the technical term given to the process of evaluation and approval. These certification bodies can thus assess and certify organizations to comply with the requirements in the ISO/IEC 20000 standard.

If an organization is verified to conform to the requirements of the ISO/IEC 20000 standard, it can be registered as such by the certification body. A certification body can be accredited by an Accreditation Body that has been acknowledged by ISO. A certification body can offer its services in any country, whether it is accredited or not.

For information on accredited certification bodies you can contact your local Accreditation Body. All Accreditation Bodies work conform the ISO 17011 standard and have joined the International Accreditation Forum (IAF). A list of all Accreditation Bodies can be found at www.iaf.nu.

6.2 Bibliography

ISO/IEC 20000 standard is composed of two parts, under the general title Information Technology - Service Management:
- **Part 1: Specification** (the Standard); published as ISO/IEC 20000-1: 2005. This is the formal specification of the standard.
- **Part 2: Code of practice**; published as ISO/IEC 20000-2: 2005. This described the best practices for the service management processes within the scope of the formal standard.

6.3 How and where to buy the ISO/IEC 20000 series

The ISO/IEC 20000 publications can be obtained directly from the ISO bookshop, from any national standards body, from several itSMF chapters, or through regular bookshops.

6.4 Terminology and definitions

ISO/IEC 20000 uses many of the terms and definitions from ITIL. The main terms and definitions used in ISO/IEC 20000 are listed in this appendix.

TERM	ISO/IEC 20000 DEFINITION
Availability	ability of a component or service to perform its required function at a stated instant or over a stated period of time NOTE: Availability is usually expressed as a ratio of the time that the service is actually available for use by the business to the agreed service hours.
Baseline	snapshot of the state of a service or a individual configuration items at a point in time
Change Record	record containing details of which configuration items (see 2.4) are affected and how they are affected by an authorized change
Configuration Item (CI)	component of an infrastructure or an item which is, or will be, under the control of configuration management NOTE: Configuration items may vary widely in complexity, size and type, ranging from an entire system including all hardware, software and documentation, to a single module or a minor hardware component.
Configuration Management Database (CMDB)	database containing all the relevant details of each configuration items and details of the important relationships between them

Document	information and its supporting medium NOTE 1: In this standard, records are distinguished from documents by the fact that they function as evidence of activities, rather than evidence of intentions. NOTE 2: Examples of documents include policy statements, plans, procedures, service level agreements and contracts.
Incident	any event which is not part of the standard operation of a service and which causes or may cause an interruption to, or a reduction in, the quality of that service NOTE: This may include request questions such as "How do I...?" calls.
Problem	unknown underlying cause of one or more incidents
Record	document stating results achieved or providing evidence of activities performed NOTE 1: In this standard, records are distinguished from documents by the fact that they function as evidence of activities, rather than evidence of intentions. NOTE 2: Examples of records include audit reports, requests for change, incident reports, individual training records and invoices sent to customers.
Release	collection of new and/or changed configuration items which are tested and introduced into the live environment together
Request for Change (RfC)	form or screen used to record details of a request for a change to any configuration item within a service or infrastructure
Service desk	customer facing support group who do a high proportion of the total support work
Service Level Agreement (SLA)	written agreement between a service provider and a customer that documents services and agreed service levels
Service management	management of services to meet the business requirements
Service provider	the organization aiming to achieve ISO/IEC 20000

Alles over de
uitgaven van
Van Haren Publishing
zie:
www.vanharen.net

Bestsellers in the ITSM Library

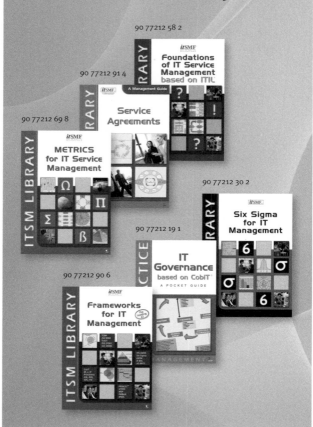

90 77212 58 2

*it*SMF
Foundations of IT Service Management based on ITIL

90 77212 91 4

*it*SMF
A Management Guide
Service Agreements

90 77212 69 8

*it*SMF
METRICS for IT Service Management

90 77212 30 2

*it*SMF
Six Sigma for IT Management

90 77212 19 1

IT Governance based on CobiT
A POCKET GUIDE

90 77212 90 6

*it*SMF
Frameworks for IT Management